From the Heart

Dianne M. Tarpy

D1564932

First Edition

Book 1 - The series From the Heart

Book cover and interior formatting by SusanasBooks LLC

From the Heart art - Haley Althea Phillips

Photographs by Howie Kra, Alex Mason, Kelly Thomas Poyner, Salisburysunrises.com, Lisa Schemerhorn, Cortlandt Schuyler, Lisa Smith, Kerri Spinazola, and Dianne M. Tarpy.
Published by Bradford Beech Tree Publishing
United States of America.

Diannemtarpyauthor.com
From the Heart – Diannemtarpy – Facebook
Diannemtarpyauthor - Instagram
All rights reserved.
Print ISBN: 9781736633205

#fromtheheart

Dianne Tarpy: Featured Poet of
Week 10

Author Tia B.

EDITOR. POET. PUBLISHER.

Dedication

I dedicate this book to those who came before me, who made a difference to others by writing words of hope and inspiration. To people who understand and feel the pain that others suffer; to those who care; to those whose journey is ongoing. As I stand on the shoulders of others, I hope that someday those who are new will stand on mine.

It is my hope that those who read this book will be inspired to share love in the many places it can be found. To find the beauty and joy even when it is difficult. To make simple that which is; to not overcomplicate life. To understand first how people think and why. To always look for the silver lining.

To remember to change the things we can to make our world better. And never, ever forget those events and times when we were at our worst; while celebrating those times we were at our best. My wish is that we find a way to create more of them.

Contents

Foreword

Just when you need it most, Dianne's beautiful poems reach out like a much-needed hug, a nod of understanding, a shared moment of awe and appreciation, and sometimes that gentle push we all need to not give up and keep on going.

From Dianne's heart to yours, each poem is a loving sacred messenger. Feeling a little discouraged or uninspired? Take a moment to think about what you need right now, say a prayer for guidance, and then randomly open From the Heart to any page. I know without a doubt that the poem you land on will be just what your heart needed to hear.

Natalie Eve Marquis
A Painter of Sacred Messengers
NatalieMarquis.com

When I first met Dianne at a youth basketball game, I immediately noticed how engaging and supportive she was of all the kids. I had the pleasure of getting to know her over the years while her grandson, Tyler, and my son, Dallion, were teammates. She would always greet my family with a smile and genuine warmth. The more I got to know Dianne, the more I grew to admire her.

Her love for family and life is extraordinary. Dianne's passion for helping is admirable and infectious. Her contributions to humanity continue with this inspirational collection of poetry. Her poems display life lessons, positivity and motivational words.

I'm so honored that she chose me to write a foreword. This means more to me than can be described. I'm humbled and honored to be a part of your journey Dianne!

Wallace Johnson, Author
20/20 Division

Dianne and I completed our graduate studies in 2010, and during our capstone week at Norwich University, I experienced first hand her sweet disposition. She nurtured all of us, her cohorts, and was always ready to lend a hand or provide inspiration.

It is no surprise that Dianne has crafted a collection of poems that almost read like a daily devotional. I can picture her sitting by the water's edge early in the morning, pen in hand, the words flowing smoothly unto the paper, like a prayer. Her poems are not just a personal prayer, but a prayer for the world; indeed, words of comfort.

I'm proud to be a small part of bringing this book to her friends worldwide. I know you will keep this book handy - perhaps on your nightstand or by your favorite chair. The poems will be there, waiting for you when you need them the most.

Susana Jiménez-Mueller, Author and Podcaster
Like Finding Water in the Desert - A memoir
The Green Plantain - The Cuban Stories Project Podcast
susanasbooks.com

Preface

From the Heart was a result of the Covid 19 pandemic and the long periods of time that resulted due to the forced isolation and resulting grief that our world experienced. Grief for those who died; for those who suffered; for those who remain, still affected by this dreaded time. It is during this time that I fell in love with the process of poetry writing.

This book is intended to soothe the soul and the heart of the reader, and bring them to a place where hope continues to lead the way; to help them believe in themselves and their ability to cope with the disappointments that life often brings.

I sat most mornings looking out my window wondering what the new day would bring. The time spent reflecting and wondering resulted in the poems you find within these pages. Along with words, I used pictures taken by myself, or my friends to further describe my feelings. I am happy to say I have many new best friends as a result of this effort. If I found a picture that resonated with me, I would ask permission to use it. I shall be forever grateful to them as these pictures in and of themselves are worthy of being published. However, it was cost prohibitive to do so. You will see a few in each chapter that represents the beauty to which I write.

These simple words, my first attempt at poetry, are truly written *From the Heart*. The more I write, the more I feel that I have found my true destiny in life. It has been the easiest thing I have ever done!

The encouragement I receive from others - poets, friends and family- spurs me on to write even more. I promise you, my readers, I shall continue on to write words of hope and inspiration that soothe the soul and heal the heart.

Dianne M. Tarpy
Haverhill, Massachusetts
February 2, 2021

Acknowledgments

I am thankful to my extended groups of friends and family, led by the entire Tarpy/Beckford clans, whose true love and respect provided me the ultimate inspiration which allowed these words to flow. My heartfelt gratitude to each of you who mean so much. My heart is full due to your support, along with your likes and loves, as I began my writing journey.

Special thanks to my husband Jim and children Gregg, Eric and Melissa, along with my daughters-in-law, Stacey and Christina, whom I cherish. I know I have done something right when I look at our three children and realize the wonderful people they have become. To my eight grandchildren, whose future I hope is brighter due to my writing, I adore you all. Each one of you are special. I seek always to see the world through your eyes.

A special mention of gratitude to Denise, Gregg, Eric, Tyler, Kyle, Lilly, and Kerri, along with my village of Facebook friends - you know who you are - who seldom missed a day of liking, loving, or commenting on my writing on social media, where this all began. Your consistent support was all the inspiration I needed to write this book. You will never fully realize how much this simple gesture meant to me.

To Gregg for creating my website: how wonderfully humble, smart, generous, and giving you are! To Eric for your daily calls on the way to work and words of encouragement, please know this is often the best five minutes of the day. To my sister Dorianne and her daughter Sarah for being my beta readers and editors, my heartfelt thanks, You two are wonderful writers. I believe I shall be reading a book that you author someday.

To my photographer friends who provided me inspiration from which my words flowed freely, I shall be indebted to you always for saying "Yes, you may use my pictures." They are Howie Kra, Alex Mason, Kelly Thomas Poyner, Salisburysunrises.com, Lisa Schemerhorn, Cortlandt Schuyler, Lisa Smith, and Kerri Spinazola. The picture on the front cover was taken at my grandson Tyler's birthday dinner on July 3, 2020, when I promised myself that I would write this book of poetry. I am thankful for that moment.

I would be remiss if I did not include my author friends whose assistance, help, and encouragement were directly responsible for the creation of *From the Heart*. They are: Susana Mueller, owner of Susanasbooks, who created the cover and supported me graciously and admirably through the formatting and technical requirements. Natalie Marquis, whose creative artistic approach to how I should organize this book during our frequent lunches kept me focused, and Wallace Johnson, author of 2020 Division, who made me believe I could do it, because he did. I cherish your collective friendships and involvement.

1 - Words Straight from the Heart

"And now here is my secret, a very simple secret. It is only with the heart that one can see rightly; what is essential is invisible to the eye." — Antoine de Saint-Exupéry, The Little Prince

This is the beginning. The place that's deep within. Where all my words have meaning and flow easily off my pen, each of them begin and end in the heart where the feelings are real.

The Park Bench

It is from the park bench
Located beautifully by the sea
That I think of the possibilities
Of life that is yet to be.

What more is it that
I still have yet to do?
What will mean the most to me?
What difference can I make?
For myself and others
Who I have yet to meet?

It is the wisdom of my years
That fuels my fire and lets me know
I am limited only by my dreams
And the actions I have yet to take.

So, my message here to others
Is that it is never, ever, too late
To do the things that will
Make a difference in your
Hometown or your state.

From the Heart

Continue on, do your thing,
Whatever it may be
Find your very own park bench
Explore the possibilities
Make those hopes and
Dreams come true
As it is never, ever, too late.

Dianne M. Tarpy

Words from the Heart

Words, wisdom and poetry
To help calm our soul
And soothe our heart.

Where do we
Find the inner peace
That calms our weary soul?

Where do we find
Those words that
Soothe our painful, broken heart?

We find them deep within
When we are very still
When the quiet comes.

From Deep within
Our mind
Our thoughts
Our heart.

These are words that never get old
They take many shapes and forms
Stories

From the Heart

Poetry
Prose
Songs.
Many that have been heard before
Some that are brand new
My hope is that they will forever
Be told again and again and again.

These words that come straight
From the heart
To calm our weary soul
And soothe our painful heart.

Why do I Write?

I write to soothe the soul
Yours and mine
To keep our hearts
In tune.

I write because there are so
Many words to be used
So many things to be said
Thoughts to be verbalized.

I write because it is important.
As a means of communication
And to reach each other
At the deepest place
At the core of their being.

I write to inspire
To motivate
To teach
To heal
To bring understanding
For myself and others.

From the Heart

I write because I care
About my family
About my friends
About those around me
Those I know
Those who are yet to be
My new best friends.

I write from the heart
Hoping that my words bring
Happiness
Love
Joy
And understanding.
I write...

So Many Words

So many
Just like stars up in the sky
From which to choose
Where shall I ever start
Will I catch that shooting star?

Love.
These words are easy.
And are used by all in life
They roll off our tongues gently
And give us all the feels
Which give our lives true meaning.

Encouragement.
It is so important
Those words are desperately needed by those who seek
To improve and find success
No matter what the goal.

Anger.
The words spoken in this way can be damaging and
hurtful.
Causing tears and pain
And can negatively affect people straight to the core of

their Being.
Denial.
Now these are the words that can strike us down.
The ones that make a fool of us all.
As we can rationalize any situation or
Refuse to admit the truth or
Even its existence.

Words.
They all have meaning.
And as a writer, they can be formed quickly,
as they seep quietly from our souls, appearing on the page.
With a beginning but no ending as there is much that must be told.

Although the four I mention here are certainly very special:
Love, encouragement, anger, denial
Because they run us through the gamut of feelings.
Just like stars up in the sky,
There are many from which to choose.
Still, there are many words we need to know,
As we learn, experience life and grow.

Dianne M. Tarpy

It is Only With the Heart

It is only with the heart
That one can truly feel
Those things that are
Essential to our soul
The ones that warm us to the core.

The ones that mean the most:
Love.
Joy.
Happiness.
Know it is these things
I will always wish for you.

As sure as the universe is moving
Along with the sun and the moon
My heart will always be with you
Today and every day.

No matter where you are
Whether near or far away.

100 Days Away From 2021

You may find this hard to believe
We are 100 days away from 2021
What is your plan for the rest of the year?

What is it that one thing
You most want to do?
The action that you will take
To make your heart fill with joy
That will make your dreams
Come true?

Whatever it is
Begin today
Right at this very moment
There is no better time
To do those things that
Make you happy
That you've always wanted to do.

It doesn't come without some work
You know that in advance
Try new ways to get there
That place you want to be
The possibilities are endless

From the Heart

No limits here, you see.
100 Days...what will you do?

While there may be mountains
In the way that you will have to climb
To make your wild and crazy
Hopes and dreams come true
Remember that
You only have
One important, precious life
100 days - what will you do?

Dianne M. Tarpy

Silver Bullet

As the sun sets on another beautiful day, I think
Where is that silver bullet I have always heard about?
One that is a simple solution
to all our complicated problems?

I've waited for it patiently but as the
time goes by I haven't found it.
Now I sit in doubt.
Okay. Well, today is a blank slate.
I can begin again.

I won't let the past take up today's energy
or rely only on fate
From a full heart I will give
All I have and start again
Create the story I've always wanted.

Affirm that which is critical to success
Refuse to bring attention to the negative.
Join me here and now
Make your decisions based on fact.

What one improvement can you make today?
That makes today better than yesterday?

From the Heart

Return to now. No matter what.
Align thoughts with what you want
Know consistency beats intensity
Mind the truth that makes you happy, wise, and healthy.

Stay focused on the solution.
Work hard and put in the time
Make choices to support your truth
And before you know it, it will be yours, unfurled
Right before your eyes.

For I am here to tell you it is
these actions it will take
because this is what I've learned (sadly)
there is no magic
silver bullet
upon which you can depend
to solve life's common problems
It takes hard work and discipline.

2 - The Times of my Life

"Life is about time. Spend more time than you do money on others. Give time more than any other gift. Also, take time when you need to. Take time for you when you need it. Sometimes time is all we have with the people we love the most. I ask you to slow down in life. To take your time, but don't waste it." — Emma Heatherington, The Legacy of Lucy Harte

It is through the lens of life that my poems are written. Sometimes a single moment; most often an experience. All share the fact that they are the words that articulate what surfaced and have become now memories.

Dianne M. Tarpy

Nineteen Years Since 9/11

How could that possibly be true
That's how many years
It has been since 9/11/01?
I shall never forget
what happened on that day,
As I was in NYC meeting with one of Verizon's best
presidents
On the 40th floor
At 1095 Avenue of the Americas
At 8:00 AM.
That day was one of the longest that I have ever spent
It was a life-altering,
life-defining moment as I
Worked to make sense
Of all that had ultimately transpired.
Hearing first the news that something horrible happened
And then seeing that smoke-
That horrific view and
war-like scenario
right before my eyes
from the 41st floor of 1095
was mind-blowing to say the least.
It permanently resides
in my mind's eye
A view I will never forget.
Working side by side with my colleagues,
we worked hard to restore the network as quickly as we
could.

From the Heart

The thought that is still with me to this day
 is how everyone pulled together and
did all they could to make a difference for themselves,
their company and
their nation.
The stories - oh, the stories!
There are many that I could share
But suffice to say so have many others who were there on
that fateful day.
I sat with all the leaders who planned the best way
through for 40 days and many long nights the
rehab of Manhattan, piece by piece,
Beginning with the financial sector
Where we all had much to lose.
What I best remember all these years later was that we
never, ever stopped
until our tasks were complete - it was April or May I
think-
Before business returned to normal and we got back to
our routine.
A promise I made to myself
As I went through this ordeal was
That I would honor all the lives lost
For the rest of my entire life
By volunteering and giving back
In my hometown community.
As we all take pause on the anniversary of this tragedy
I shall always remember my colleagues and my friends
who worked side by side with me,
in the worst of times

doing all they possibly could
to restore the network and get
NYC communications back.
But most of all, my thoughts will be
With the families
as I mourn with them the loss
of all the people who perished
Workers. Firefighters.
Police. EMTs.
I shall forever hold
a special place
in my heart that aches
in my mind that will
Never Forget
what happened on this day.

New England Summer Storm

Lightning flashes
It fills the sky
Thunder crashes shortly after
Rolling on and on and on
We know it will stop eventually.
Getting darker by the moment
Even though it is only 5:00 PM
It is a summer thunder storm
That is sometimes scary but beautiful still.
But the storm is oh so welcomed!
For it breaks the cycle of
humidity and heat
Bringing us the soft rain,
crisp air, and soft breeze.
It is only us true New Englander's
who can appreciate and realize
That it will make our breathing
And living so much easier.
Four seasons
Presented to us in different ways
The change of weather they
Offer just when we think we've had enough,
is appreciated.
Winter, spring summer and fall
Each have their own beauty
And offer something different.
I am grateful for them all.

Dianne M. Tarpy

Like Sand Through an Hourglass

So go the days of our lives...
It has been said by some that
Old people live in the past.
Young people live in the future.
Wise people live in the present.
This I know for sure
Time is never promised
Or even guaranteed
Time cannot be stopped
No matter how hard we try
Once the sand inside the hour glass
Moves through and hits the bottom
We cannot pause it or get it back
Or save it for another day.
Time is a precious resource
I believe on that we can all agree
Understanding this perspective
Will help us all to learn to be
Living fully in the present
Taking advantage of every day
And the moments it presents to us
And also, along the way
Providing all the wisdom needed
to make our choices right.
As these choices will keep us forever
healthy, happy and strong
With open arms to seize the day
Making good use of the time we are given,
for it is truly a precious gift

From the Heart

And are the keys that will provide us
A life of much personal success.
These are also the truths that will protect
the integrity of our life
and serve to keep us on the path
to make our life fulfilled.
On these words I do thee promise
you can always depend
But, for now I will leave you
as I started:
That as sand through an hour glass,
So goes the days of our lives...

Dianne M. Tarpy

Calm and Patience

Calm is important in our environment today
and patience is a virtue they say
Two things that are sorely needed
In our world as it revolves around us
With constant twists and turns
While we all await the news.
Record voting was what it took
The choice to many was clear
As they did their civic duty
By working at the polls
Voting for their party
Or holding signs outside.
No matter what transpires
My hope for all is this:
That our country comes together
Understanding that
calm and patience will serve
All well this year.
That collectively we will continue on
Wishing that things will now
Be better as we begin anew
With respect for one and all.
That we all learn and listen to those
who seek to teach.

From the Heart

Understanding what
we already know:
The United States of America
Is - and always - will be
the home of the free and the brave
Where our flag shall forever wave!

Dianne M. Tarpy

Enjoy the Moments as they Happen

Enjoy the moment
The big guy says
Be grateful for the opportunity
To play a game you love.

Remembering the highlights
Of those games played
along the way
That will forever stay implanted
In your heart and in your mind.

Many take for granted the physical
Attributes required:
The shot
The quickness
The mental toughness
And the amount of practice
needed to get those
skills down pat.

The team-mates who are now
best friends whose backs
you'll always have
Who teach us
the importance
Of commitment and
what it really means
To work hard, never give up, and
do that one more rep.

From the Heart

Being relentless in the
quest for excellence
Step right up to meet that mark
"We always touch the lines."

Enjoy these games
and moments as they happen
For they are fleeting, that's for sure
Before you know it, the time has passed and only
memories remain.

Dianne M. Tarpy

A Beautiful Start to the Day on the Lake

Sunrise on the lake in Maine
Is such a peaceful experience
The birds are chirping all over
Singing tunes that are pleasing to hear
It is the only noise it seems that's coming to my ears.

Other than the stillness around me
(Wait - is stillness not a sound?)
It is so very quiet
Remarkable actually
All is well in this world I have found.

The lake is as smooth as a mirror
With a few ripples here and there
The sun reflecting in all its glory
Burning the fog off the lake silently
It is a beautiful start to the day.

It's moments like this
we take for granted
And don't appreciate its inherent true worth
For it is certainly priceless
A sight to behold for all time.

I promise myself to take note of
How much beauty there is in it all
To take pause and truly be thankful
For although it is only a moment
It is one I will treasure for sure.

From the Heart

Dianne M. Tarpy

A Moment in Time That Warms the Heart

There are moments in time
that will stay with you forever
that you'll never forget and
carry deep within your heart.

Capture these moments
whenever you can
as they become the
foundation of memories
for years to come.

These are events
that warm our heart
sometimes they are very simple
sometimes they are
milestone events.

One thing for sure is this, I know
these times of our life
though some may seem
mundane must be duly
recorded in our
hearts and in our minds.

These moments are precious
the memories that result
are to be appreciated
and never forgotten.

From the Heart

Take the picture
write the poem
put it in a journal
capture the memories somehow
to ensure they are
carried deep within our hearts
where they'll be with us forever as
a moment in time that warms the heart.

3 - Words of Inspiration and Hope

"We must accept finite disappointment but never lose infinite hope."
—Martin Luther King, Jr

These are words of inspiration that are meant to bring you to that place where dreams come true. The intent of this chapter is to help you get there, to that place you want to be.

Dianne M. Tarpy

I Shall be One...

I shall be one who sees
The beauty in every day
In the sunset and in the sunrise
In the blue sky and in the clouds.

I shall be one who forgives
And moves on from all those things
That bring pain and discomfort
Dark times and disappointment.

I shall be one who looks for the good
In every person, place, and thing
Hoping always that it is right
As the good is always there.

I shall be one who seeks to understand in spite of all
The discontent and rage
Knowing that it will bring me to
That place where peace resides.

I shall be one who cares
And hope that those who see
Will join me in my quest to
Care about each other as
Kindness is important to longevity.

From the Heart

I shall be one who takes pause to appreciate
The beauty in every day we live
To forgive is where it's at
To always look for the good.

I shall be one who seeks to feel while
Caring for all people
Myself and my fellowman.
While taking time to say,
simply, to myself
Sometime during every day
I shall be one...

Dianne M. Tarpy

Where are you on your Mountain?

The climb is often tough
Sometimes I have to stop
Take a breath and be thankful
For the view I see at the top.

I have worked so hard to get here
To that place I want to be
It is clear that I am not done yet
As I still have many more steps
To climb
Right in front of me.

I don't give myself enough credit
I often sell myself short
Not realizing that I am worthy
That all my small wins have value
They will get me to the top.

It is with this open mindset and
a renewed belief in self
I will move slowly forward
and continue on
As my journey has momentum
and the mountain top seems near.

I shall appreciate each step I take
And each person I meet along the way,
as they become fond memories that help me
reach the destination before me.

From the Heart

I am here to tell you that
you, too, can make the climb.

First, find your own mountain
Fix it squarely in your mind
Have your faith and belief
in self firmly aligned
With the realization
that your time has finally come
Your mountain is awaiting you
Your journey has begun!

Consistency In What We Think and Do

When we stop re-reading
the last chapter of our life,
We can begin to write a new one
It is this I am sure of.

What is it that you dream of?
What is your vision of success?
Close your eyes for just a moment
See that version of them
both in your mind's eye.

One important component
of success is consistency
We must be consistent
in all we think and do.

Let's make it our mantra to embrace
the words that are written next:
-Show up (be where your feet are)
-Repeat (consistency)
-Grow (success)
It matters not what was done before
the past is not your friend.
As I have often heard the ship doesn't sail
on yesterday's wind.

Don't be afraid to start again
And push yourself even further
Each action that you take

From the Heart

Every twist and turn along the path
Puts you closer to your goal.
Even though you may not know
what's waiting next around the bend
You will never lose, I promise that
You will either learn or win.

Dianne M. Tarpy

Good - Better - Best - You are Free to Choose!

Another day we are given
and this is what I've learned
It's all about decisions
The ones we make each day
That shape our world
And our lives
For better or for worse.

The challenges we face
Are most often difficult
How can we handle
overcoming obstacles
and find the best solutions?

We have to meet them head-on
And not settle for just the good
Or simply just the better
Strive to achieve what's best.

The best choice
Which leads to
The best decisions
that are possible for you.

Good-better-best you are
free to choose;
Don't just settle for the easiest
Choose what's best for you.

Disappointment

How often in our life has disappointment found us?
This emotion can often be buried deep
Within our hearts and minds
and can sometimes knock us off our feet.

Like much of life, when disappointment hits,
we feel like failures, internalizing the feeling
Wish we had done better
and tend to get in a rut.

I say, on this day,
To give yourself a break.
You have been working hard
Did your best
Gave it all you had
So, to yourself be kind.

Because on the other side of this sadness
And feelings of disappointment
Are success and happiness, just waiting to be found.

Dianne M. Tarpy

Today YES, I CAN!

Here we go.
Today's the day!

As I stop and take a moment
To figure out what I can do
To make life even better
I think about the need to be consistent in all I do.

It is the "yes I can" mentality
that will help achieve my goals
And also facing the reality
that it is really all up to me.

What one improvement can I make
That makes today better than yesterday?
Today I shall align my thoughts with
what I truly want the most.

Returning to the now with things
Because yesterday and the past
Matters not in the scheme of things.
I am finally on my way.

With an open mindset
and eyes looking towards success,
the affirmation stated simply,
"yes, I can" planted firmly in my head
I shall be moving forward
working hard to win the day!

From the Heart

Dianne M. Tarpy

When Wishes and Dreams Come True

What could possibly compare to this day?
The beauty it brings
As I sit and watch the day begin
I am struck by what it presents.

No better picture could I paint
To compare to the reality before me
Even though our lives aren't perfect
It is days like this that motivate
And cheer us on. Don't blink.

As the day passes far too quickly
We must admire the here and now
Knowing that living in the present
And the decisions that we make
Are what is most important.

It is at the in between place
where the sand meets the water, and
the water the sky, and
the sky the clouds,
that peace and tranquility resides.

Dreams may be found here.
Enjoy this day.
And every day presented to you.

From the Heart

As it comes your way,
Find the good and make it great
Knowing you have the power
Within your heart and mind
To make your wishes and your dreams come true
As I see mine, right before my eyes.

4 - Blessings Abound

"When you arise in the morning, think of what a precious privilege it is to be alive -to breathe, to think, to enjoy, to love." — Marcus Aurelius

These are what I wish for every day for me and you. They are the very simple things that are right before our eyes. Find them in your own back yard. Appreciate and know they have been there forever, just waiting to be found. These are the blessings of a grateful life.

Dianne M. Tarpy

The Beauty of a Beech Tree

Shall I ever see
Anything as beautiful as this tree?
With branches reaching tall into the sky
and leaves that rustle softly
in the breeze.

With color that compliments
The world around it
With a smooth gray bark
And leaves of mahogany.

A tree that never, ever disappoints
One of the first to sprout its' buds
And holds its leaves until late fall
With a shape that rivals no other.

I shall be thankful
For nature's finest product
Knowing that in New England
We are blessed
With many others like it.

But often we are too busy
To take the time to see
What things we have
of great beauty
Growing right before our eyes.

The Beach On a Warm October Day

It is only in New England
on a warm October day
we can be out on the
coastal beaches with the
Sun and surf and clouds.

Being oh so very thankful for this gift
a day that is so beautiful
and totally not the norm.

As I sit here by the ocean
I understand why writers choose it
as a location to spend time
where the thoughts flow so easily
into words, forming poems before my eyes.

The environment is so peaceful
The sound the water makes
Is music to my ears, as it
Forms the beautiful waves
And the breeze blows ever so
softly through my hair.

The familiar smell of that salt air
brings me back to when I was small and
unaware of all that the ocean gives,
asking nothing in return.

Dianne M. Tarpy

It is the place that we can go
when troubles come our way
And nothing seems to be going right.

As after spending time here
You cannot help but feel
Better and blessed for the experience
It really can help heal.

This to you I promise:
Visiting the beach will help to clear your mind
Soothe your soul completely
Help you to search for new meaning
Which leads to finding the answers
Wiping out the uncertainty and sadness
so prevalent of late
While helping to make things right
again for all within your world.

The Why of Your Journey

As you begin your journey
Someone is offering help
The universe is supporting it all.

You must do the work
That is part of the trial
The physical and mental changes
That result will be the reward.

The transformation is real
Making your time count
The journey is incredible
For those who will succeed.

Good health is the bonus
Behavior modification is the key
What do I need to proceed?

Set a goal with systems in place
That will provide a life of success
Give it a value that's important
That can be achieved no matter what.

Live a life of significance
With structure, gratitude and appreciation
As all of it is important.
Never forget the why of your journey.

Dianne M. Tarpy

Looking to the future
To see what you want to be
Do it for 30 days
A habit then is formed.
Take it to 90 days.
It is there a lifestyle is found.

My True Blessings

I am thankful
When I stop and take a moment
To fully realize
The beauty of time
spent together
With people I idolize.

I am truly thankful
For these times that mean so much
And grateful for the opportunities
That life seems to always present.

To celebrate occasions
Whether big milestones or small
With our family and friends
means far more to me
than they will ever know.

I am grateful for each one of them
Understanding how it is difficult
To bring them all together
Makes it even that more special
Because they always seem to manage
To find a way to make it happen.

Dianne M. Tarpy

So, as this life of ours passes on,
And the weeks turn into years,
I shall look to find more reasons
to celebrate these milestones big and small
As it provides our life true meaning,
presenting memories and blessings
to cherish for one and all.

Blessings by the Sea

No matter how many times
I come here, to the beach nearby my home,
I marvel at the beauty that it presents to me.
it is indeed a blessing
to have it so close by
a place where all is welcoming
there are no frustrations here.

Life and power are in our hands
to do whatever we wish as
everything seems possible here,
no failures to be had.

The secret of finding happiness is this, I know:
to sit here by the sea and
count my blessings, being
grateful for them all.

While others are sitting elsewhere and
adding up their troubles
Which makes so little sense
As it brings them only more distress
with feelings of discontent.

So, it is to the beach I'll go
- Or anywhere near the water -
Where blessings flow and gratefulness abounds
in my mind and in my soul.

Dianne M. Tarpy

"The deeper the cry, the more clear the choice."
- Mark Nepo

Don't debate the choice.
You know what needs to be done.
Half of life's success
is in the choosing
The other half is in understanding.

The question we must ourselves: how deep within is our
cry?
Does this choice
align with our purpose
And fulfill our life's desires?

When sitting in this mindset
And searching deep within your soul
The cry becomes much quieter
The choice becomes so clear.

We know it won't be easy
None of us expected it to be
That which we promise
Ourselves is the thing
that matters most.

Dianne M. Tarpy

"Yes, I can" is my mantra
This I know to be true
My words to myself come from
A deep place of truth and wisdom
where the choice is more clear.

Good health is what will bring me
To that place of happiness
Making good food choices
Along with some exercise
Is the path that will get me there.

poem inspired by Elizabeth Benton

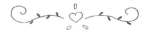

5 - Today is a Special Day

"Learn from yesterday, live for today, hope for tomorrow. The important thing is not to stop questioning." — Albert Einstein

The promise that today will bring should never be underestimated. As we live and breathe yet another day, it always starts anew, allowing us to experience the best that life can give.

Dianne M. Tarpy

The Power of the Morning

A new day.
New beginnings.
The morning contains new possibilities
We can start, yet again, to be all we would like to be.
Don't give up.
No matter what the past delivered.
It is today that you will say
"Yes, I can."
Take advantage of all the tools
That you have before you
Be here and now
With the knowledge
That perfection is not the goal
Participating is the key
Let's together pull towards that we seek
Good health
Great joy
Continued happiness
There is power in the morning
Today will be your day!

The Beauty of the Sunrise

Oh, how beautiful the sunrise!

The colors running through the sky
In anticipation of the revealing
Even though we've seen it often
Each one is more awesome
than the one before.

The reds and pinks before us lay
And then the fiery ball of yellow
The sun displays itself silently
So round and strong and bright.

Reflecting on the water
It presents before our eyes a vision
And a sight to behold for all time
One to cherish and behold.

It promises us another day
To be and do whatever we wish
A clean slate of opportunity
To find whatever it is we seek
Fulfilling all our hopes and dreams
That are close within our reach.

Dianne M. Tarpy

Seek Peace in Every Day

Seeking peace, one often must start early
As it is when the day is most quiet.
A treasure can be found by those who do
Along with the beauty it presents.

A location by the sea often is that place
As it brings people together
Each in their own way,
In their own time.

No need for words.
Or justification.
Or action.
Stop.
Sit.
Enjoy.

The true beauty of our world
Can be found in the day
No matter where we are.

The reward is great
At a price we can all afford
Whether by the sea
Or in the pasture
Or in a slow and winding road
Or in the mountains.

From the Heart

The true beauty of the day is yours
Just waiting to be found
Today, find that treasure
Whereever you may be
Make today a good one
One you shall remember by
Taking pause to appreciate the
Beauty and peace
Which can be found in every day.

Dianne M. Tarpy

Embrace the Wait

In time, all things will happen
Just as our universe expects
However, it never does as quickly
as we would like it to.

When nothing is certain
Anything is possible.
Let that sink in.
What does that mean for you?
What is that one thing you wish for?

Today, be patient.
You are worthy of your dreams
Know that they will happen.
That you are capable.

When you put in the effort,
Do the work,
Pay the price,
Easy is earned.

In the end, the reward will be exactly
what you wish for, if you embrace the wait.

Today Is Where You Need to Live

A new season begins
The leaves begin to show their colors
The morning air is crisp
Time for new beginnings.

What direction are you going in today?
Forward!

Know that living in the past
Doesn't help
You are better served
To learn from it
Move forward
Be smart.

Live in the moment
Make good choices today.
Today is where you need to live.
Forward is the next destination.

One of Those Days

Did you ever have one of those days?
When nothing goes as planned
The sadness creeps in
The heartache feels so real
Yet there is nothing
That can be done.

Or is there?

In times like these we must
Continue on.
Move Forward.
Control the controllable.
Believe.
This, too, shall pass.

From the Heart

Dianne M. Tarpy

Today is a Gift

What is it about today?
That makes it very special?
Perhaps it is because the sky is blue
And sun is shining brightly?
Or is it because you are feeling great
And want to keep the feeling going?

Whatever it is continue on
For you see, today is a gift.
No matter what the weather
Or your state of mind.

This gift of today is given freely
So, use it purposely
Live, laugh and love others
Make a difference where you can.

For the events of today that transpire
Will quickly turn into memories
Experiences that will serve you well
Appreciating all that life has to offer.

As you look back you will be glad
That you did not miss the good times
And all that that this new day brings.

From the Heart

Accept the invitation
Take those pictures now
Go on the trip even if it is last minute
Knowing the best is yet to come
Realizing all the while that today is a gift and
Possibilities are without end.

Dianne M. Tarpy

Be Thankful for This Day

Welcome your day from a place of peace
As the dawn sheds light on the day and the sun rises
Be aware
Of all that life has given
Of the beauty that the day presents
Of the love you have deep in your heart
For yourself and those around you
Be thankful
For this day
As it will never come again.

6 - Grateful for this Moment

"Thankfulness is the beginning of gratitude. Gratitude is the completion of thankfulness. Thankfulness may consist merely of words. Gratitude is shown in acts." — Henri Frederic Amiel

I have never fully realized the beauty and joy that gratitude offers. It has been only when I stop and pause to reflect on simple things that I find them, those things I often took for granted.

Dianne M. Tarpy

Mornings

Yet another.
Quiet.
Peaceful.
The beginning to
Another day.
For this I am thankful.
For the promise it offers.
For the gift of life.
I will not take for granted
The opportunities it presents to me.
I shall make good use
Of the moments.
Of these mornings.

Life by my Window

As I sit by my window many thoughts go through my
head.
I watch as the season changes
Having more time than I normally do.

These are crazy times.
A pandemic they are calling it.
Days that lead to nights
Nothing is the same
People are angry and want it to stop.

What can I do? How can I help?
Stay home! Wear a mask! Stay six feet away!
Wash your hands!
It is all so simple, or so it appears.

I can do all those things, can't I?
To protect myself and those I love?
My friends, my neighbors and strangers alike?
For sure, I promise to do my best.

As I sit by my window one thing is for certain:
I can. And I will. This too shall pass.
But more important than doing it
Is how it gets done.

Dianne M. Tarpy

I promise to do these things with
Kindness and grace in my heart.
Thankful for what life has given me.

All while hoping that the anger
I see in many begins to dissipate
And the kindness then can start.

Your Destiny is Here and Now

Have you ever had these feelings?

These moments of destiny

When you know
that you were
meant to be right here.

At this place.

At this time.

Doing this very thing that life has offered you today.

Some may feel that it is the
moment for which we were created
A destiny or fate
that serves us well and
then becomes a path leading us on our journey
to what all along was
life's purpose and reason for being.

Be grateful for this feeling.
It may be your path to success paved by:

Contentment
Happiness
Peace.

This is your time. Your destiny.

Dianne M. Tarpy

Cherished Moments By the Sea

These moments by the sea
on a warm October day bring an incredible
warm feeling that all will be okay.

We take these simple moments
That are given to us so often
Without full realization of
how important they can be.

Instead of giving full appreciation
For their worth and the
role they play
in keeping our minds and hearts
fully in tune and engaged.

As the years go quickly by me
I shall enjoy each day to
its fullest
understanding the importance that
every hour can deliver.

Each moment, experience
and event is something to behold
As the years now pass like weeks and
the weeks go by like days.

I will now
Take nothing for granted
As I realize the worth of it all

One thing, for sure, is this I know
These moments by the sea
are the ones I will cherish most of all.

A Brief Time

When all things are considered
Our time on this planet is brief
Understanding this we need to
learn to be better
With our actions and our words.

Using words that make
others happy and always being kind
helps to take away the sadness
In our hearts and in our minds.

Being grateful for the moments
Helps us all move forward towards
A life well-lived, allowing us
To make the most of every day.

Putting worry behind us
Thinking positive is where it's at
Knowing that this type of thinking
Will help to make life worth living
And this brief time on earth fulfilling.

Dianne M. Tarpy

Moments Between A Mother and A Son

It is these special moments
Between a Mother and a Son
That will live forever
To remember and to love.

They do not seem to happen
Often enough
As we are all so very busy
With our lives, our jobs, and stuff.

So, when they do,
We must take pause and appreciate
These times that seldom come our way
To ensure they stay forever
In our hearts and in our minds.

When the moments are
Captured by a picture,
On the dock at Goose Pond,
Surrounded by sky and nature
It serves to make the experience
Even that more special
One that everyone will remember
For some time to come.

The Second Best Time Is Now

"The best time to plant a tree was 20 years ago.
The second- best time is now." — Chinese proverb.

Now.

What will your now bring today?
Whatever that is:
Execute.
Give your best.
Think big.
Restart.
Begin again with that
which is most important
These simple terms speak volumes
and will move you toward success
in your chosen endeavors

Dianne M. Tarpy

My Own Back Yard

As the day ends
And the night falls upon our land
I take a ride and realize the beauty
that before us lies, taking pause for
gratitude and reflection.

At the end of my street
Is a farm with a huge field,
With a white barn that can
be seen in the distance.

The sun is setting behind it
It is a sight to behold
In this moment, I marvel at the beauty
that our neighborhood possesses.

I am thankful that I have realized
- Just now -
That a view I have witnessed thousands of times
I have never taken time to give its proper due.

I must remind myself to
do this more often
Stop and take moments like this
to fully appreciate the beauty

Offered by places nearby
This is just one of many
impressive locations I have
in my own back yard.

I encourage you to do the same
Take the time to look around
With eyes that look to find
And to fully appreciate
The beauty you have in
your own back yard.

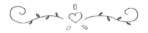

7 - Living a Life of Peace

"If you love peace, then hate injustice, hate tyranny, hate greed — but hate these things in yourself, not in another." — Mahatma Gandhi

Living a life of peace is truly a thing to behold. Giving the space and grace to appreciate all that life can offer. Sometimes good. Sometimes difficult. Embracing all that is presented, knowing the difficulty will pass. Which brings us back to that place of peace where all is right in our world.

Dianne M. Tarpy

Living a Life of Peace

As I sit by the lake and wonder
What is the best I can do for myself?
How can I get where I want to be?
What I have learned is that
Life can be simple.

It doesn't have to be complicated
There is beauty all around
us everywhere I look.

It is here by the water that I believe
I have figured it out:
Stop negotiating with yourself
Entertain no other option
Work hard towards the life you wish.

Once your mindset is wide open and
The due diligence has been done
You will have achieved your
Life-long mission of living
the life you wish.

Fill it with all that means
the most to you
Surrounded by good health
Wealth and happiness
It's here that the good life
can be found
A life of peace and love.

From the Heart

Dianne M. Tarpy

A Time for Silence

We know there is a time and
Place for everything
Many times, we have been told.

Have we thought about the
Need for silence
And what it means in our daily life?

Taking a moment to be quiet
Sitting alone with our thoughts
Can help start a day fully vested
In ourselves and our fellow man.

Taking this moment out in nature
Can triple the effect it will make
In our minds and our hearts,
Of this I am certain
As I have experienced it first-hand.

Anywhere near the water
Or in a forest with the trees
Watching the stars or the
Clouds in the sky
Means so very much to me.

So, I suggest you take pause
At some point during your day
Whatever works the best for you
It is the simple act of doing it
Actually following through.

From the Heart

It will certainly improve your life and
Help to clear your mind if you
Make it a priority-
Setting a space daily for
A time
For silence.

Dianne M. Tarpy

Space and Grace / Time and Place

As we begin another day
We must do a better job
Of understanding the importance of
Space and Grace
Time and Place.

Space to give people a chance to think about what is said
Space to rethink is it necessary?
Is there a better way?

Grace to give the benefit of the doubt we have
In ourselves.
In others.
With our points of view.

Courteous goodwill
We all deserve that, don't we?
Time is sometimes needed before we hit that button;
Or say the words we will regret,
Once heard they aren't easily forgotten.

There is a Place for everything that transpires in this
world
It is an important piece of how it's received
And the consideration it's given.
So let's move forward accepting
That all are very important

From the Heart

Space and Grace
Time and Place.
Given and received
To each other as human beings.
Know we all
Really mean well,
but simply have differing
points of view.

Accepting that it is okay
As none of us is the same.
Space and Grace
Time and Place.
All to be considered.

Dianne M. Tarpy

Last day

It is our last day in paradise.
A pretty one it is.
On the Cape Cod Shore
Where the water is warm
And the sun is plentiful.
As the sun begins to rise
and quiet fills the air
The possibilities presented
are front and center in my mind.
Another chapter closed in the summer of 2020
Where the unexpected happened
More times than we can count.
Today I will
Let my mind be free
Let worries float away
and things that seem of great concern
can quickly disappear.
Taking a deep breath
And letting it slowly go
Will serve to
Let those stress-filled thoughts
Lift quietly from my head.

From the Heart

I can fully appreciate
all that this day offers
Along with much
Good health,
much joy, and continued
happiness
on our last day
In paradise.

Dianne M. Tarpy

Life's A Journey

While we know that life's a journey
There's a whole lot happening in our world today
Some things that make no sense
Yet somehow, we must continue on
Find ways to cope and
work through it
Even in the face of
sadness
disappointment
and
discontent.

There is no other way to handle
All that comes our way of late
I refuse to call it fate.

Because I believe that
good is waiting
Right within our reach.
We must believe
There is a way
To live our lives these days.

In the face of all that causes pain
We need to know for sure
That with faith and
Belief in self and others
We will be okay.

From the Heart

We will turn this all around, you see,
And live life as it was meant to be for
ourselves and all the others.

We will make this world of ours a
place where can be found
Peace and love for family, friends and
our fellow mankind.

Dianne M. Tarpy

Embrace the Grey Sky Days

Embrace the grey sky days
They are good
For our soul
For our mental health
For the rest they can provide.

Every day is important
Whether sun or rain or grey
As they give us opportunities
To be all that we can be
Which helps to find life's purpose.

These grey days give us extra time
to calm the mind
Reflect on life
Contemplate
Find the good in the stillness.

Listen.
To your mind.
To your heart.
Invite here the full truth.

It's here that you will find the
love and joy
That fills our heart with peace
And fills our days with purpose.

Cloudy Day

Cloudy, cold and rainy
But even on this day
We can be thankful
For the possibilities it presents.

The ocean is still performing
Big waves and sounds and beauty
That will never go away no matter what
The weather forecast or the type of day.

As the wave recedes
let your troubles too,
washed swiftly away by the water
as you learn by not validating the problem
but finding instead the solution.

As we seek the change that makes
us better by taking proper action
and making better choices,
We can't forget that along the way
Our thoughts, feelings and
behaviors also come in to play.

It doesn't have to be all or nothing
In a world where so much is absolute
Today explore the middle
Find your change that makes sense
Searching to find that mid ground
where happiness and peace reside.

Dianne M. Tarpy

This, Too, Shall Pass

This, too, shall pass.
It must.
As it can't get any worse
Our world is upside down
The hurt
The pain
The disregard for one another.
It will get better.
It must.
We have put in our time.
Paid our dues.
We are better humans than this.
I know
the positives outweigh the negatives.
It's just right now everything is not as it should be.
It will get better.
I have faith and believe.
It is a privilege to
Live kindly and serve others
For the good of the whole.
Use your words
To heal and help
Individually and collectively

From the Heart

We can and will
move past this craziness.
"Let there be
peace on earth
and let it begin
with me."

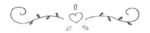

8 - Love will Bring us Together

"Raise your words, not your voice, it is rain that grows flowers, not thunder." — Rumi, The Love Poems of Rumi

It is the never-ending circle of life that's filled with love. Both of which are necessary and upon which we all depend. Love is as necessary as the air we breathe in order to prosper and grow. Love is needed to achieve the success we search for in our life.

Dianne M. Tarpy

I am Always With You

You can find me in the stillness of the morning
you can find me in the sound of the wind
the rustling of the leaves
in the calmness of a soft spring rain.
I am always with you.
you can find me
always deep within your heart
where the love resides
and your soul is found
I shall, forever and always
be with you
this I promise you.

What is the Purpose of Today?

To Love. To laugh. To find the joy.
To find the things that make us smile
Knowing that some days are easier than others.

Realizing that life doesn't give us
all we want
but always all
we need.

Finding purpose in today?
Even through a pandemic, you may ask?
How can that be possible to do?
I know. You're right.

It isn't easy. It is difficult for sure.
"Control the controllable" I've often said.
But this pandemic is one of those things
far beyond our reach, at times it seems
At the moment, anyway.

We have to do our best
to handle
the fear and uncertainty
while finding methods and ways to cope,
to help us muddle through.

Dianne M. Tarpy

As I begin to start the day
I shall always be sure to remember
To search for purpose
no matter what it is
that life decides to deliver.

To love, to laugh. To find the joy.
Shall be my mantra always, in good times and in bad
Although I may, of late it seems,
need much help to find it along the way.

Silver Lining

Where is that silver lining?
That one we all look for
When the chips are down
When things seem bad
And
Our life is turned upside down?

It is the optimist within me
That keeps me feeling strong
With knowledge that
As long as I do not quit
These things will turn around.

I refuse to think negatively
I expect the best to happen
In life for ourselves and others
Because I believe in silver linings
I know they will occur.

It may not happen
as quickly as wished for
With a timeline that is rigidly set
But I promise it will come to fruition
If you agree to commit.

With patience, love and positivity
In your life and in your thoughts
You will find that silver lining
The one we all look for.

Cry A Tear or Two

I shall cry a tear or two
For the story that is yet untold
The one that caused your heart to break
and cause unhappiness.

I shall cry a tear or two and stand
Beside you as
Your dreams are shattered
into pieces right before my eyes.

I shall cry a tear or two and
hold your hand throughout
The whole ordeal as it plays out
And causes so much pain.

Please also know that
this, too, shall pass;
And I will be there for you then
And move with you through the
sadness and the pain
To the other side
where light and love reside.

I will cry a tear or two but what
will be different at this time
Is that they will be
Tears of joy and happiness
With smiles and gratitude.

Dianne M. Tarpy

The fact remains that
no matter what,
I will be there by your side
In good times or in bad times
With much love for you forever
In my heart will always be.

Saturday, June 20, 2020, 100 Days

100 Days
Thank you, my friends
(you know who you are)
should I miss a name or two,
for following me the last 100 days
And sharing your
likes and your loves.

Taking the time to read what I wrote
Letting me know that you found
Worth in the words.
Leaving a comment,
or remark or message
Means more than you can ever imagine.

You have given me hope
Brought a smile to my face
As I worked diligently
to get through
the days.

Your kindness and caring
I will always remember
And for good measure
For you, I have done:

Dianne M. Tarpy

Carved a special place
Deep within my heart
As I am
humbled and gratefully touched.

That you took a moment
To read, to like, to love, to comment
My words that came straight
From the Heart.

The Path to a Life Well Lived

I am thankful for this day.
For the love of my family
For the beauty the day brings
For life.

I am thankful for the ability to be
Here and now on the shore of
South Yarmouth, Massachusetts
To experience the expanse of
Sun
Sky
Sand
And marvel at it all.

Taking life as it comes.
Being grateful
Always appreciating what I have
Always looking for the good
In people
In experiences
In places.

I shall remain thankful and grateful
For these simple things
All the days of my life.

Understanding they are the path
to a life well lived;
filled with
good health,
happiness and
love.

The Circle of Life

As we grow and learn together
One thing I know for sure
We are more alike than different
In these times which are like a blur.
As we grow and learn together
One thing I know for sure
We must walk the path of what is
right and just doing what we can.
As we grow and learn together
One thing I know for sure
Love will win the battle
Much sooner than living in fear.
As we grow and learn together
One thing I know for sure
The Circle of Life becomes evident
When we take the time to listen
Being present for each other
In perfect harmony.

Epilogue

If my book *From the Heart* makes a difference in one person's life, I will feel I have achieved my goal. It is my hope that these words of inspiration, written in this uncertain time of a pandemic, will bring hope and healing to the world, by soothing one's souls and hearts.

About the Author

Dianne M. Tarpy is an author who is late to the scene of poetry writing, having worked in the corporate telecommunications environment for over 34 years. In this role, she experienced first-hand the life-altering tragedy of 9/11 in New York City and the resulting aftermath and restoration of the network. She is a community and family-focused leader, resident, and hometown sports fan from Haverhill, Massachusetts, where she has lived her entire life. As a wife, mother of three, and Nana to eight beautiful grandchildren, she has lived long enough to experience life at its best and its worst. Having achieved two master's degrees, she is the recipient of a number of awards at the national and local level for her work achieved in giving back to the community in which she lives and works. A voracious, lifelong reader, writing has always come easy. Little did she know that lying quietly within her was a book waiting to be written - she just needed the right time and mental space to do so. The silver lining of the pandemic is that she feels as though her life's purpose has been realized. She believes in learning that never ends and knows that one person can – and does – make a difference. As well as knowing that it is never too late to do or be all that you wish for.

Made in United States
North Haven, CT
29 January 2023